Obituary

A Collection of Poetry

Jamie L. Reeves

Obituary

A Collection of Poetry

Jamie L. Reeves

ISBN 13: 978-1-955338-32-5

Kristin Martin, Editor,
Cover background, Canva-design by Jamie Reeves,
Lori Graham, Book Designer
Printed in the United States of America

pp

POCAHONTAS PRESS

Floyd, VA
pocahontaspress.com

Dedicated to my sister, Dani,
who I will miss forever.

For 15-year-old Jamie,
who needed these words
long before they were written.

For Riley and Avery,
who gifted me sisterhood
when I feared it was lost.

Table of Contents

I DAUGHTER

II SISTER

III WOMAN

I

DAUGHTER

Young Mother

I'll never see the path my mother walked
in early mornings on her way to school.
I'll never live in Chicago,
or know which path she took and why.

My mother in 1985 is something
that I would kill to see—
13 years old, searching for a hairbrush,
running late…

I won't get to ride in the passenger seat
of the car she drove to school
when she turned 15.
I'll never really know that by then
she started skipping class
and drove to work to pay the bills.

My mother in 1987 is a girl
stronger than I've had to be—
Raising her own mother, cooking dinner,
smoking cigarettes…

I don't get to know what my mother was thinking
on her way to the hospital.
I'll never know if she was happy or distraught
to be having my oldest sister,
or if she liked that it was one week
before her 18th birthday.

Sometimes I need my mother in 1989
more than my mother now—
Before five children, a failed marriage, bad knees…

God Is a Woman, and She Is My Mother

I'm afraid one day
my life will be split into two—
a before and an after.

My mother's love—
and after she's gone.

As a child, I thought my mother was God.
Her words were truth,
and I loved no one more.

Her heartache made the clouds cry,
and the sun only shone when she smiled.

After my mother is gone,
I don't know who I'll believe in.

Daughterhood

Daughters are extensions of their mothers…

You are her—
crying into your pillowcase
when Daddy screams over spilled milk.

You are her—
blowing cigarette smoke out the window
when the tears dry.

You share her nightstand
with Prozac secreted in the drawer,
and her cold shower—
(because everyone else comes first.)

Daddy

Why do you lie?
Tell me, Daddy,
what's in your drink that gives you the right?

Daddy lied again today.
He swore we'd play outside,
but it poured and the wind was so brutal,
that I worried it would carry me away
and never bring me back.

I didn't see the sun for days,
and Daddy stayed away.

Babe

Daddy cut the knots out of my twisted hair,
and held my hand so I wouldn't suck my thumb.

I sucked my thumb until I was nine,
and I was twelve when he paid for the braces
that fixed my gapped teeth.

All the stocking stuffers and Easter baskets
Daddy paid for never amounted to
the love I had for him.

I'll always be the little girl
sitting in his lap as he trims my nails,
and the little girl who forgives him
when he cuts them too short.

Confessions

Some nights I find myself
smoking pot in the bathroom
of my two-bedroom apartment.
Lately, it's been more often than not.

The window is open,
the fan is on,
and I'm still terrified of getting caught.

I have to remind myself
that mom isn't down the hall,
and dad isn't in the bedroom next to mine.

I feel I'm staying up too late on a school night,
like I'm in the wrong house
and need to yell for my parents
because they aren't here to hold me.

I wonder if their separate bedrooms
feel as far apart as the miles
that separates me from them.

I think about calling them to confess…
but I save us both the trouble.

Once More

Mom, can I sleep in your bed tonight?

Grab a string and pull my tooth out;
I want to see the fairy once more.

I won't stay up late on Christmas Eve;
you can leave the presents
and I'll pretend I don't know.

I know I'm bigger now,
but I promise I'll share the blanket.

Yell at me to clean my room.
Buckle me into my car seat.
Console me when I scrape my knee—
you never were afraid to touch the blood.

I'm growing very tired,
and I need my mother's warmth.

I want back into the womb.
I want to do it all over again with you.
I want to be a Girl Scout again.

(Or maybe I just want to be a girl.)

Mom, I want to sleep in your bed tonight
and wake up when the blue jays sing.

Those Before

The women who raised me
have the strength of a thousand men.
They have bodies as powerful as oxen,
minds as resourceful as honeybees,
and hearts pure as children's.

Mothers, sisters, daughters, and wives—
but above all else, they are women.
They are survivors of men,
and a world designed against them.

Bear children.
Provide comfort.
Put others above all else—
the expectations of womanhood.

Be gentle.
Be warm.
Be modest—
feminine assumptions.

The women who raised me
taught me about choice—
that womanhood and femininity
are just words to men,
but choices for us.

That choosing myself is not a selfish act,
And to be warm does not mean
I may never be cold.

II

SISTER

Riley

I played my favorite song
on the speakers in my room.
My little sister listened against my door,
and I heard her humming the tune
for the rest of the day.

I stood in front of the bathroom mirror
and applied my burgundy-colored lipstick.
She came in behind me,
holding her cherry ChapStick.

I took her with me to the salon,
and she watched as I browsed the polish colors.
We walked out with matching nails.

She breathes the same air as me
and follows every step I take.

So, when I tell my mother that I hate her,
she mimics my words,
and I feel I have handed her a gun.

I sit her down, trying to empty the bullets
and explain to her that she can't say
such hateful things.

"But you did," she says.

Dirt

I remember when the dirt was fresh,
when the soil felt moist,
and there was nothing yet signifying
that this is where she would lie to rest.

I remember the gash in my heart
and its battle to pump blood
throughout my veins.

The air was humid; it was July.

The aroma of the thorny roses
placed on her chestnut-colored casket
seemed to rise through the ground.

(Or maybe it was the marigolds
on the stranger's tombstone next to her.)

Her funeral was a koi pond,
crowded with faces fused together.
All I know is that I don't see any of them
now that the dirt is dry.

They don't sit with me on the
two-thousand-day-old soil
covered with grass that goes uncut
for far too long.

I wonder if they've seen
her dark granite tombstone
that has July 16th engraved twice.

My heart is doing the best it can
since I stitched it up with string
from arts and crafts,
but I still find the wound
more opened than closed.

And the blood-red roses I leave behind
for her always die too soon,
because, although it always
feels like July, it's not.

Happy Deathday

This year, my birthday is on a Tuesday.
A Monday would be horrible,
but the weekend would be great.

Tuesday doesn't mean anything to me.
My birthday doesn't mean anything to me;
and I try to forget that I have one.

My sister died on her birthday.
Mom always said she put us into the world
and could take us out.

But really, that's what God does.
Whenever he wants, wishes, or feels compelled to.

Tuesday is a very boring day for a birthday,
an even more boring day to die on.
My sister died on a Monday, and that was horrible.

Reasons

I would drive the long, gravel road to the church
only to scream at the sky.

I didn't know where to place my anger,
and the box I kept it locked in
was beginning to wear down.

I hadn't prayed in years,
but I needed a reason.

The response— the echo of my own voice.

I was the only one who could find a reason
that would satisfy my grief.

My heart began to repair,
and my screams grew quieter
when I realized that Death is all that is fair;
it does not pick favorites.

I don't know why Death chose her so soon—
I don't think there was any reason.

Reassurance

I wanted to hold you
like the sky holds the ocean.

I wanted to crawl into your skin
and become you—
mimic you in every way.

I didn't know how else to keep you alive,
but your skin was too cold,
and I was already forgetting.

That night, I dreamt I had found you.
You drank from the river where you bathed—
it was always clean.

Heaven was kind to you.
I lost you in the colors
that my eyes couldn't comprehend.

Keep going, you said to me.
Your soul found a place to stay alive.

Last Request

Sometimes I worry that I might be a killer.
My fear isn't that I have sinned—
only that I'm slowly killing what is left of you.

I don't mean to murder your memory.
The pieces of you don't fit together anymore,
and every picture is blurred.

I promise: Father Time made me do it.
I'm wrongfully convicted.

Let me be free— take me where you are.

I want to feel what it's like
to remember again.

Brother Bear

The brother I see at Christmas dinner
isn't the same boy I played with after
opening presents in 2008.

He doesn't look or talk the same.
His hands are much bigger now,
but his chin is still scarred from
the basketball incident.

Sometimes I look at him
and all I see is the shell of a man,
and it's hard to believe that
he's the same boy I once knew.

I loved my brother then, and I still do.
But he isn't the boy that I shared timeouts
and backseat car rides with.

When I was seven, he taught me
how to snap my fingers and count to one hundred.
At nine, he started covering my ears when
my parents yelled things I wasn't supposed to hear.
In 2008, he held the scissors
that opened our toys from Santa.

Sometimes I cover my own ears
and pretend I'm in his room again,
before we moved out and before we knew
the cracks in the house weren't from age.

I think about calling him
and telling him that I forgot how to snap,
so he can teach me all over again.

I want to share with him the weight I carry,
and tell him how life is harder now
that there are no presents for us at Christmas.

I miss my brother, the one who always
played with me even when he got too old.
I miss being his best friend, his favorite girl.

I used to cry when he wasn't near me
and count the minutes until he came back.

But now, when I see him at Christmas,
the presents aren't for us,
and it isn't 2008 anymore.

Sister, Mother

You'll never know it, but Mom
grew too tired to be your tooth fairy.
You came along just as she ran out of magic.

As a child, I filled your stocking
on Christmas Eve shortly after
I had tucked you into bed.

I hid eggs in the yard on Easter morning,
not understanding how you believed
it could be a rabbit, but not me.

I held your hand across the street
to trick-or-treat, then checked your candies
before you ate them.

Mom drove the car,
but I walked you into school.
She bought the ingredients,
but I made your dinner plate.

Too young, too careless, too out of touch—
but still, you could have called me mother.

Avery

I had never seen a baby girl that didn't cry.
You held in your tears fiercely,
as if you owed the world for being alive.

You're only a baby;
the worries aren't yours to hold,
and the grief can wait.

Enjoy being little and alive.
The eyebags from your nightmares
will soon be replaced with smile lines
from your daydreams.

25, 15

My sister, it's time to let go.
The ten-year age gap between us
wasn't the only tear in our relationship,
and I'm tired of pretending it was.
I've had enough of crying on the car ride home
and when I lay on the grass atop your grave.

Still, in both cases,
I try to imagine you as if
you were holding my hand.
I try to feel the lines on your palms
and the bones beneath your knuckles.
I try to get a sense of the woman I knew
rather than the one I hold responsible.

Your absence has made you easier to blame.
You robbed my final years of childhood,
you stole what was left of my naivete,
you loosened the screws that held our family intact,
but worse—
you died, and now I will miss you forever.

No matter where I search,
I will never find you in anyone else.
Sister, you are invaluable and haunting.

I've dyed my hair black for years
so that I resemble you.
Since I can't turn to you,
I look for your features in the mirror.
I trace the lines on my face
and hope they'll lead back to you.

Everything leads back to you—
from the way I tie my shoes,
to the rotten milk in the refrigerator,
left behind when the power shut off
and the bill went unpaid.

If only there were somewhere
we could hide together,
and I'd never have to pay another bill
or feel what it's like to miss you.

We could live there forever,
where I am five and you are fifteen.
You'll pour my morning cereal
while I admire the clothes you wear
and your long, silk, jet-black hair.

Flowers

Rain falls to feed the roots below.
The sun unfolds the petals.
Waste recycles into resources—
billions of years of repeated patterns.

They bloom every spring:
chrysanthemums, dahlias,
marigolds, and orchids—
but the most beautiful thing
lives beneath the ground,
and was returned to the Earth
the day they buried you.

III

WOMAN

20

I am twenty years old.
I work,
go to college,
feed the cat,
grocery shop,
pay bills,
and brush my teeth twice a day.

Throughout every action of every day,
I imagine what I was doing ten years ago.

Tonight, I will wash my face
with a $40 cleanser,
while ten-year-old me
is desperately trying
to pull out a loose tooth,
in hopes of earning five dollars.

After breakfast, I will Google
"therapists in my area"
and read into which one is best.

Ten-year-old me
is busy determining
which blue crayon colors water best:
Cerulean,
Navy Blue,
maybe *Aquamarine,*
certainly not *Sky Blue.*

After trial and error,
she decides on
Pacific Blue,
since she remembers learning
the names of the oceans.

This is how I will spend my twenties.
I don't see any other way.

Somewhere, Anywhere

I want to move somewhere far away—
so far that I leave myself behind.
The town I'm from holds nothing but graves
and family-owned burial plots.

I want to meet new people,
in a city like New York,
or rent an apartment in Chicago,
where my parents met and fell in love.

A cottage in the country
sounds comforting—
I could imagine myself in
Maine or Montana.

Still, I don't believe I'll ever be
satisfied with where I live.
Everywhere I am, I don't want to be.

I dread the beach because of the heat
and the sand, but I daydream of a home
with the ocean at my door.

Maybe it would take leaving for
a different country to outrun myself—
I've always felt that Italy
was calling out to me.

I need a place with no mirrors, only windows
so that I have space to breathe
without reflecting.

Is there a place I could go
where I might finally disappear?

Graduation

I finished college in the quiet of my apartment
with my dog lying at my feet.

I uploaded an essay on World War II poetry,
closed my laptop,
and realized it was over.

I hadn't made a friend in four semesters.
I never knew what to say after we finished
discussing the difficulty of the assignments.

They'd tell me they hated the professor
and that the assigned essay was losing them sleep.

I'd hide the fact that I'd imagined myself
having coffee with our professor,
and that I would write the essay an hour before
it was due, then sleep soundly.

I could never see eye to eye with anyone,
perhaps because I was avoiding eye contact.

How can I write of truth yet never speak it?

My studies have taught me much about literature
but nothing about myself.

I don't think there's a major for that.

Mountains

The highways here hold deer guts
and headlights that don't work,
but I guess it's like that
everywhere in the mountains.

I told him just the other day
that I gotta get outta here.
I kept convincing myself
that things would be better up north.

I could live by the water
and freeze my ass off in the winter,
but the snow on the mountains would be worth it.

This morning, my dog looked at me like she knew.
If she had any bags to pack,
they would've been sitting by the front door.

I asked her what she wanted.
The only thing I could hear her think was,
"Go."

I've been trying to understand Appalachia
and what it means to be a Virginian,
but every time I think about my home,
I imagine another lock
being placed on the door.

These mountains hold me close,
but they never let me go.
If I could leave, I would've left already.

The Mountain Is You

My parents told me I was just a little girl,
so I never tried to be anything else.

My siblings told me I was weak,
so I never tried to be anything else.

My friends told me I was boring,
so I never tried to be anything else.

My teachers told me I was average,
so I never tried to be anything else.

It wasn't until the words got too heavy;
I had to empty them out and start over.

By then, the only one around to tell me anything
was myself.

I told myself I was a baker
and found that muffins are best made from scratch.

I told myself I was a painter
and realized my walls were far too bare.

I told myself I was a poet
and saw that my words could move mountains.

I told myself I was enough,
and I wouldn't need to be anything else.

Mother Earth or Father God?

I want nothing from the world
and the world wants nothing to do with me.

The trees I plant from seeds I stole
won't grow until I'm long gone.

The air I breathe will be recycled;
it was never really mine.

I'll be blamed for the contaminated waters
and the cow factories, yet I don't swim,
and I've never cared much for milk.

All I own is stardust
and even that will be reused.

Everything is worse now that we're here,
and I don't know what I was made for.

The Shark at the Bottom of the Ocean

I lie in bed like a shark
at the bottom of the ocean.

The air that I breathe isn't meant to kill me,
yet the shark is consumed by the water
he once swam in.

His lifeless body sinks to depths he never knew.

He is picked at and torn apart
by the creatures he once horrified.

He would be ashamed to see himself
as he is now.

The shark on the ocean floor once felt
like he ruled the entire sea.

He didn't know his life would come to this,
that he too would feel like prey.

I burrow in my sheets and close the windows,
waiting to be consumed.

But there is no ocean floor for me to sink to,
no prey to pick me apart.

The shark will never know sunlight
or a breath of fresh air.

Once he sinks, he can never swim.
But for me, there is always tomorrow.

The Hills

I died on a hill today,
and I'll die on another tomorrow.

You'd have to pull me by my hair
to get me to come down,
or send a rescue team
into these mountains to find me.

I've died a thousand times
but I'll live a thousand more.
I have frozen, starved, suffered, died,
and decayed on these hills.

No one has ever come to save me.

The hills can be cold and lonely,
but they are built on my beliefs,
and the views are always worth it.

Promises in the Storm

I cannot meet you halfway
on a road that is broken.

I can't sail the seas to find you in the storm
if all I'm left with is half of a boat.
I refuse to cut my hands on shards of glass
when thunder shakes the house.

I cannot promise you that I will always be
loving, patient, and nurturing.
Sometimes, I will be cold, cruel,
and unrecognizable.

But I ask that when it is you who feels that way,
you take shelter underneath me.
Can you seek warmth in my embrace?

The mirror won't be shattered—only foggy.
Will you clean it and find yourself again?
If you can promise me, I will do the same.

17

It's important for me to remember
the girl I was at seventeen.

Staring at my seventeen-year-old self
wouldn't be looking into my reflection.
It would be looking into my core.

In the same way that, if you tore me apart,
you'd find my blood and organs.

Pick apart my brain, and you'd find her,
along with every version of myself—
they all still live there.

They feed me poetry,
and through it, I give them life again.

I owe that girl every breath I take,
and every word I write.

July 4th

The fireworks boom and pop,
then crackle down the night sky.
You wonder if you should
cover the dog's ears.

Somehow, she isn't bothered
and doesn't bark.
She watches the sparks and the colors
she cannot see.

She tolerates her headband
marked with stars and stripes,
but her leash is off
because she never goes far.

She eats a popsicle melting on the ground,
then lays in your lap.
She sees your joy
and licks at your knee.

A bright blue firework paints the sky
and illuminates her black fur.

The country is loud
and has a long night ahead,
but by the end of the hour,
she will lie in bed and wait for you.

The Atheist's Dilemma

Tell God that I'm ready.
Tell Him I'm done
with the empty savings account,
the dead flowers on my windowsill,
and my own reflection.

Tell Him that death can have me
and I don't want to hear it.
He can't convince me
with the promise of spring,
the coast of Virginia,
or the warmth of my mother.
I mean it, I'm done.

Death leaves no decisions.
Death won't provide answers
but neither does God.

If this is the repercussion of God's silence,
then maybe the sun shines for me and
not by His word…

Perhaps God has gone deaf—
became nothing more than a false hope,
a capitalist's dream,
or the echo of my own thoughts
searching for a reason to live.

Tell God I need more time to decide.

Cigarettes

Cigarettes make me sick,
but today I had a few.

I found a pack of Camels
on the ground outside, a full one.

I had one for breakfast, lunch, dinner,
and while I took a bath.

They made me want to throw up, cry,
change states, be a child again, and die.
(I settled on throwing up.)

My fingers still smell like smoke,
and I'm afraid my hair is ruined.

Back Home Memories

Sometimes I wish I couldn't hold on to memories.
Maybe then I wouldn't disassociate when
driving past my elementary school,
remembering that my dog's life is in my hands,
or visiting my parents.

All that I am remains in the past.
I can't focus on today or tomorrow.

When family visits get too loud,
I sink into the hole I started digging when I was nine.
I would dig each time my parents yelled,
or my brother stormed off angry,
or one of the babies got hurt.

The familiarity is comforting.
I can only sink there when I'm back at home,
but the walls were built on distress.

Sometimes I go sit outside instead.
Then the dog barks, and I'm brought back to the
graves of the pets buried in our backyard:
dogs, cats, birds, fish—
I was always sentimental.

Life seemed so short when I found out
they don't live as long as we do.
Now, all life ever seems to do is drag on.

My family home knows too much,
but my apartment knows nothing at all.

It seems unfair that no place I ever live
will truly know me,
and I'll never fully know it,
not like the house I grew up in.

When my parents told me they wrote their will,
I wasn't sure what to expect.
I didn't know who'd get the house
and all its memories.
I'm still not sure if that's something
I want to hold onto forever.

If all I know is a house full of love,
resentment, hope, and grief,
what else is there for me to learn?

So much, I believe.
But I'll never learn it
if these memories won't let me go.

Appalachia

They tell me I'm from Appalachia,
and I stare at them, confused.
I never knew there was a name
for the mountains that held me captive.

They ask me how it was to grow up in Virginia,
and I realize the thought had never
occurred to me before.
Virginia was always home,
but I spent my time between walls
and never between trees.

I wonder if I'm an Appalachian writer,
even though it took twenty years
for me to hear the mountains call out to me.
I was deaf to them before,
or maybe I was always ignoring them.

I was always trying to run away
to find a beautiful place
where life could stand still,
then one day, while I was packing my bags,
I stepped outside and found it in my backyard.

My dog was napping in the sunshine,
and my dad was firing up the grill.
My little sister bounced on the trampoline,
and the neighbors were coming over.

The mountains were the background,
and I noticed how they held us together safely.
I've started to see that they never trapped me in—
they were inviting me to stay.

How to Write a Poem

The mountain was too big to move,
so I never tried again.

The pen became too heavy
and the sheets too comfortable—
so I lay there,
ready to die and never write again.

Then I thought back to what
an English professor once told me,
"Don't get it right, get it written."

It didn't matter how many pages I threw away
or how many words I erased,
so long as I was writing.

So here I am,
getting it written and trying it again.

Dimples and Dust

Baby, I always loved your hazel eyes—
hazel like the moss that surrounds a creek,
gentle like the stream it runs into.

Baby, I know how things got to be like this—
when your soft cheeks started to hide your dimples,
and your skin began to grow cold.

Once, I held you, and now you walk the path,
the same as your sister did—
before she was gone—gone, gone, gone.

Where do people go when they're gone?
And where did my Baby go?
Gone—and you always blamed her.
Things only make so much sense to a child,
you could only take so much grief.

Baby wasn't a child for long,
because children don't know what "gone" really is.
Gone means hiding behind the door
or out for a drive.
Gone never means forever to a child.

Baby learned what gone meant
and that her knowledge made her less of a child
than the other children.

Gone, gone, gone.
The place people go when they're gone
makes them feel like stardust again—
like fragments of a being
that never really lived.

But Baby remembered who had lived
and what it meant.
Gone showed that love is strong,
no matter how weak grief made her feel.

She imagined the place being dark and empty,
but she knew stars shined bright,
and the night sky showed that
they were never alone.

Baby, it's okay.
You were always right—
gone doesn't mean forever.

The Garden

God, turn me into a flower,
since I have yet to sprout.
Let me lie under the sun
and bathe in your gracious showers.
Let the bumblebees find a use for me
that I could never find myself.

God, turn me into a flower.
Let me be beautiful in a simplistic way,
so those who pass by
can admire me as I am.
Let me smell of lavender or rose,
of honey and cut grass.

God, turn me into a flower
for I don't know how else to be.
This world has picked me apart
beyond what I can bear.
Why not let me be picked for my beauty
and nothing more?

God, turn me into a flower.
The beauty of this world
is only attainable for a season—
any longer of this vile world
and I will begin to rot.
I can no longer bear the harsh, long winters
and their crisp, splintering air.

God, turn me into a flower,
and I will never pray for anything more.
You will never see me weep or wilt;
I will only lean towards the sun
and make use of the bees.